T0327841

Herbal Magic

JOURNAL

SPELLS, RITUALS, & WRITING PROMPTS FOR THE BUDDING GREEN WITCH

THEODOSIA CORINTH

wellfleet press

Contents

Cultivating Herbal Magic

Working with herbs predates recorded history, but today you have almost limitless access to a bounty of information to explore, once available only if you grew the herbs yourself. Growing them yourself is always an option, but, as with all things magical, choose what works best for you.

In this journal, you'll find exercises and prompts for reflecting on and deepening your relationship with the herbal world. Aligned with seasonal cycles, it will help guide you through your year as a gardener and an herbal ally. It contains a plethora of spellwork, both formal and informal, to help you make the most of your herbs, whether for consumption, manifestation, or simply connecting with the earth. It doesn't contain comprehensive guides to growing or working with specific plants, but you will find tips and best practices for working with a wide variety of plants across growing zones. You also will find a rich infusion of herbal lore, magical practices such as moon cycle work and astrological correspondence, and other mystical ways to connect with the power of plants through reflection, intention, and writing.

Living your best magical life requires belief in your powers, an openness to your intuition and the messages it receives, and trust in the Universe. Tending an herbal garden or a magic life means working in rhythm and harmony with nature. It affords the opportunity to slow down and feel the sun warm your skin as you nurture the plants and connect to the soil. Water gently. Banish weeds. Tame stragglers. Celebrate bounty. Listen to your heart and hear the messages carried on the breeze. Mother Nature will not be hurried. She moves at her own pace, so delight in the cycle and trust that the seeds you plant will come to fruition.

In times of uncertainty and chaos, escaping to your herbal sanctuary—be it a forest, garden, patio, kitchen, or windowsill—and communing with the natural world, even for only a few minutes a day, can bring a sense of peace, calm, and accomplishment. As you wander your path of herbal magic, take time to be present in the moment. Set intentions and goals based on your beliefs, hopes, and desires. Draw the magic to you or send a blessing into the world—but do no harm. Plants are living, breathing beings that deserve your care and respect, and they have much to teach. They also can prove harmful if not used properly. Never touch or ingest any part of a plant (seed, fruit, flower, leaf, stem, roots) without full and proper knowledge of it and never do anything that feels intuitively wrong for you.

WHAT IS AN HERB?

The botanical definition of an herb is any seed-producing plant that doesn't have woody tissue and dies back at the end of the growing season. In the culinary world, herbs come from the leaves of a plant, while spices, usually dried and crushed, come from any other part (root, stalk, fruit, seed). In a magical apothecary, herbs include all types of plants, such as traditional herbs, spices, flowers, and even trees, all with the potential to promote bewitchery, charm, and healing.

When and how did you first realize that plants have magical properties? How did you first cultivate them in your life? If you haven't cultivated them yet, what do you hope to achieve with them? What powers do you have already that you hope to use or strengthen by forging new bonds with the herbal world?

....

....

....

....

....

....

....

....

....

....

....

....

....

Magic Tools within Reach

You already have at hand many of the tools you need for successful plant magic. Only a few seeds, a small pot of dirt, and a sunny windowsill will get you started. Just like you, a plant needs a safe place to grow, fresh air, water, and food. Its food comes from the sun and the earth; water helps it move nutrients through its body; and the vessel in which it grows helps it establish solid roots to thrive. Sometimes life really is that simple.

You will need the following everyday supplies to grow your herbal allies.

SUNLIGHT

You probably have more sunshine in your home than you realize. Spend a day or different times on different days watching how light moves through your home or surroundings. Remember to consider:

- your kitchen
- windowsills
- fire escapes
- front steps
- sidewalk areas

WATER

Many budding herbalists struggle with knowing when to water. Some plants are picky, but most herbs and edible plants want damp soil so they can use the moisture to keep themselves upright. You don't need a fancy watering can or mister. Here are a few means to ensure your plants don't get too thirsty—just make sure to clean them thoroughly!

- Detergent bottles
- Juice or milk containers
- Large water glasses
- Spray bottles
- Vases

VESSEL

Plants don't care what they grow in. If it's deep enough, with good, damp soil and the right light, a plant will thrive in any sturdy container. It doesn't even need drainage holes; just water less frequently. Some plants will sprout directly in water. Here are a few things you already have on hand that are just waiting for new occupants.

- Candle cups
- Coffee mugs
- Food containers
- Mixing bowls
- Teacups
- Tin cans
- Yogurt containers

SURFACE

Some plants need only a little light or thrive with a little help from a growing light. If you're unsure how to line up a slice of sun with a surface, try a small table or plant stand in a spot you identified in your sun scouting. Other options include:

- bathtub or shower corners
- bookcases
- cabinet tops
- shelves

If someone asked you to plant a garden in your home right now, what tools do you already have and how can you use them? Imagine sprouting cuttings in shot glasses, planting in recycled food containers, and using spoons to dig. Get creative!

If you could grow any plants in your home, what would you grow and why? Forget about climate, maintenance, or space for the moment. Think about your favorite flowers or foods and focus on what they represent and how they make you feel. Use your imagination to make a magic garden in your space.

Connecting to the Magic of Plants

Powers stir within the earth, enabling it to create an array of plants as varied as the tallest redwood to the smallest lichen; in every color of the rainbow and some in between; bitter, savory, sweet, pungent, spicy, thorny, silky, healing, mesmerizing, and more. The magic of the natural world presents itself all around you, every day, and herbs represent one small, yet mighty, component. They reveal their secrets, communicating with all your senses.

Feel the velvety touch of lamb's ear as you absorb its soft message of peace, compassion, and the importance of listening. Draw in the smell of pine and its scent of success. Behold the uplifting beauty of a rose in full bloom and contemplate its power to attract love and friendship. Hear willows sighing in the wind and let their gentle healing energy soothe you. Taste the fruit of the apple blossom, absorb its nourishing refreshment, and perhaps glimpse your true love as you close your eyes and savor its sweetness.

Blending herbal magic into your everyday life enhances your connection and communication with the earth, honors it in a positive and sustainable way, begins or expands your magical practice, and seasons your life with purpose and intention. You don't need to be a witch—green, kitchen, or otherwise, though all are welcome—to learn what herbs and their energies can bring to your world. Only your imagination can limit their versatility in magical and practical applications, so set free the magic of your mind.

Herbs aid all kinds of magical concoctions in the kitchen: baked goods, infusions, tinctures, charms, and potions. Use herbs in your spellwork, combining them with crystals and candles to enhance their vibrations and your intentions. Burn herbs or sprinkle them as an offering to cleanse and bless a space. Mark your sacred circle or decorate your altar with herbs, fresh or dried, before rituals. Herbs can honor goddesses, spirits, ancestors or even yourself in a self-care or healing ritual. Adding essential oils, the soul or essence of plants and flowers, brings forth even more magical energy.

What plants already form part of your daily routine and how? Consider all of your senses. What plants do you see every day; hear, smell, and touch outdoors; and taste at each meal?

....

....

....

....

....

....

....

....

....

....

....

....

....

....

With what plants do you already have a personal relationship—a favorite flower, a particular herb or spice, a specific tree or shrub. Why do you feel strongly about these plants? Describe your relationship with them below.

Herbs, like flowers, can represent people, places, or memories. Think about those that you hold dear in your life. How are herbs connected to your special moments? Do you relate any specific herbs with special people?

Channeling the Life Energy of Plants

Before diving into spellwork with your herbs, attuning yourself to the spirits of plants can help you recharge, like a chat with a close friend. Growing or working with them might be just what you need.

A walk among herbal companions allows you to be alone with your thoughts but not alone in the world. Studies have shown that spending time in nature has a measurably positive effect, but you can undertake the following guided journey from the comfort of your bed, chair, porch, or patio. No wildwood or garden necessary. This visualization can take you from wherever you are to as far as you want to go. It can ground you, energize you, or strengthen your powers.

If you can, walk outside in a park, your neighborhood, a garden, yard, or any meaningful patch of green. If you're taking this journey indoors, tending to your plants and herbs, use this walk as a guided meditation. A conversation with Mother Nature is the finest kind of therapy, so put on your shoes or make yourself comfortable as you begin.

GUIDED VISUALIZATION

Take a deep, cleansing breath, in and out, fully aware of your breath.
Focus on how your body feels as it breathes in nourishing oxygen
and releases stress and tension on the exhale. Visualize your muscles
relaxing and feel yourself become lighter. Listen for the quiet. Breathe
until you feel fully present in the moment, with no worries on your mind.

As you continue to breathe, imagine that you're in a soothing,
friendly forest with trees of all sorts towering over a garden path.
Look up, down, and all around. Notice the details of your vision. As
you walk the path, you spot in the distance a beautiful blooming herb
garden. Before you focus on the garden, notice the trees that line the
path. Attune to their spirit. Can you hear their leaves rustle? What are
they saying to you? Do the trees provide shade, or are you walking
in sunshine because their leaves have fallen? Is the air cool or warm,
damp or dry? Can you feel the energy of the wind on your face? If it feels
good, pause for a moment to enjoy the sensation. Can you smell the
trees welcoming you? Feel their energy fill your heart.

Are birds singing in the trees? Can you identify any by song, color,
or shape? Listen for a moment to find a call and response. That pair of
birds is watching over you. What are their songs saying?

As you continue along the path, how does the ground feel beneath your feet? Is the path smooth, rocky, gnarled with roots? With each step, connect to the earth's energy. Feel it charge through your legs and into your torso, increasing your pace toward the garden. Give thanks to the earth for her support in all things and pledge to continue to sustain her.

As you emerge from the forest and approach the garden, what other plants can you see along the path? Is blooming clover nodding cheerfully in the grass? Is an overgrown rose bush beckoning you with its scent? Are bees buzzing nearby? Do you see a mossy step, a jack-in-the pulpit, willows waving hello, a gentle brook? Listen to the water as it runs along its bed. Put your hand in the water. Feel its cooling energy infuse your skin. What plants are growing along the edge of the brook? You are in no hurry. All is good. You are here. It is joy. Breathe and believe.

When you're ready, continue to the garden. It's in full bloom, and the energy and scents in it are intoxicating. What can you smell?

This is the garden of your dreams, containing every plant you love, lush, healthy, in full flower. What do you spy first? See it in detail. Note its size and shape. Describe its color and texture. Inhale and exhale. How does it smell?

Walk through the garden, visualizing your favorite plants as you go. Pause along the way to see, smell, touch, and feel thoroughly connected to your garden. What do you say to the plants? What do they reply? Have you found your favorite yet? What is it? How does it feel to see it thriving so beautifully? Thank the garden for the beauty and energy that it gives to your life.

Now it's time to return home, but you can come back here anytime you like. On the journey home, relive the peaceful, nurturing, connecting emotions that you felt in the garden and the forest. As you do, affirm that you, too, are thriving beautifully in this world and that your gifts have much to offer. Delight in the possibilities and offer thanks for the opportunities to grow and nurture along the way. Like the plants, you are a creature of the earth and one of her greatest accomplishments.

I ask the Sun and Moon to bless these seeds I wish to grow.

To warm and coax, encourage, and feed to spread their roots below,

while reaching limbs to Sun-filled skies and welcoming the rain.

Abundant harvest, lush and strong, each herb sings its refrain.

When you picture your ideal natural place to wander, where is it and what does it contain? Describe what you visualized in the guided visualization and what emotions it produced for you.

Incorporating Herbs into Everyday Life

ven if you're just starting your journey of discovery, you already are an herbalist. How? You likely have been using herbs your whole life, be it chamomile in a cup of tea or basil in pesto. It doesn't matter if you've purchased these items rather than grown them from scratch in a garden. An herb is an herb. Don't let self-appointed gatekeepers make you feel that, to have the greenest thumb, you must grow every herbal ally yourself for your magic practice.

That said, a special relationship does develop with an herb when you bring more intention to how you connect with it, and you can do so in lots of ways. You can buy fresh herbs for cooking and drying. You can buy herbs from smaller growers, a Community Supported Agriculture (CSA), farmers' markets, or local herbalist shops. You can focus on the sustainability of your consumption and what you use, choosing what grows well locally or even foraging for your own wild plants. (If you choose this last option, consult with local experts and pay attention to their guidelines to avoid harm to yourself or your local wild places.)

The best way to start is by choosing a specific goal: local, sustainable, self-grown, foraged, or just exploring a particular herb's many uses. Think of it as a guiding star and work toward going as deeply as you can, increasing your knowledge and intention with every opportunity to use a particular herbal ally. Focus on the relationship you build with that plant and keep notes on it if possible. You'll find acting in this more intentional way with already-familiar herbs just as helpful in creating an herbalism practice as exploring new allies.

Good herbs do join this fearsome fight

to keep my worthy goals in sight

and wick away the habits rued that fail to help me win the right

to cheer and brag when I am through, each hope and dream

achieving true.

What are the most familiar herbal allies in your kitchen, self-care rituals, or spellwork? Which have you always wanted to explore? List your favorites, any that you want to try in your practices, and why.

Guidelines for Herbal Magic

When using herbs to conjure magic, you must follow only two rules. First, do no harm—to yourself, others, or Mother Earth. Second, know your plants. Without the long history of herbal healing, modern medicine wouldn't exist today, but you must research herbal practices carefully and speak to your medical professional(s) before embarking on any herbal treatment to ensure that it doesn't cause harm or interfere with your health or existing care routine. Legions of information are available, but deep knowledge and wisdom are required. Similarly, many of the herbs within these pages have culinary properties, but you should consume nothing without fully understanding its true identification and properties.

With those caveats in mind, here are some tips for herbal magic success:

- Be intentional and sustainable in selecting, growing, harvesting, and using your herbs.

- Respect Mother Earth and all her inhabitants.

- Let your intuition guide your herbal magic practice and relationship with the Universe.

- Work with the seasons to honor the natural cycles.

- Use natural elements in your herbal magic as much as possible.

- Honor the plants that you harvest and use them with gratitude for the energies they provide.

- Practice patience.

- Believe in the power you possess when you combine intention with words and herbal energy.

*What herbal practices already form part of your daily life? What
rituals or traditions do you want to learn about and try for yourself?*

SPRING

With new warmth and new life, spring brims with exciting developments as the days lengthen and plants awaken. Humans feel the impact of longer days as much as other animals and plants do and awaken to a new sense of hope and inspiration. If you're already a gardener, you likely have spent winter considering what you want to plant. If you're newer to plants and herbs, you likely have been dreaming of green leaves and the ability to leave the house without wearing gloves.

Full of potential energy, spring represents a special kind of new year for magic practitioners, when the cycle of life renews itself. It's a wonderful time to make plans, invest energy in new habits, and set intentions for how you want to spend your time in the sun. It requires patience and hard work to tend to the seeds you plant. They don't sprout immediately, and they require energy and resources to grow and flourish. That time is also a time of observing, listening, and learning about the world around you.

Let's look at the basics of planting and the foundations of engaging with an herbal garden, including how you can work with it for protection, boundaries, and intention-setting and reflect on how to deepen your relationship with plants as both of you grow.

A Guide
to Garden Basics

HEED THE SUN

Before you plant anything into your garden, keep an eye on the day star for a while. Note where the frost dissipates first and where it stays shady and cool. Due to orientation and sun exposure, every space has microclimates, and the rest of the local environment influences it as well. Some of your plants will thrive in full sun all day, and some need the protection of shade to stay sweet and tender.

FEED THE DIRT

You can buy potting soil or raised bed soil easily at garden centers or hardware stores, but the dirt in the ground contains so much more than you think: mycorrhiza, other helpful fungi, leaf mold, compost, wood chips and grit, fertilizer, and even stones. Depending on the plants, you should prepare their homes beyond just a bag of dirt. Don't use potting soil with vermiculite or perlite for anything planted directly into the soil; these mineral additives don't decompose. Always use the right soil for the right task.

KEEP WATER FLOWING

One of the most important aspects of gardening is making sure your plants are irrigated properly. For those growing in pots and containers, that means a regular watering schedule to keep the soil moist, which can call for twice a day in full sun to once a week for cool, shady areas. Indoor plants' needs also shift with the seasons, so an inexpensive moisture meter might help if you're worrying about over- or under-watering.

LOOK FOR PATTERNS

Every garden is unique, and it often takes trial and error to find just the right place and plant. This process offers one of the joys of gardening, but if you feel impatient, keep a daily or weekly journal of what you've tried and what works so you can build your knowledge constantly. If you pay attention, no one will know what's better for your garden than you.

KEEP LEARNING

There's always more to discover when growing herbs. Sun, water, seed, and soil may seem simple in theory, but there's infinite variety in what you can learn. Let your curiosity and enthusiasm guide you. Pick favorites and let what's special and exciting to you sweep you away. You'll be following the footsteps of every green thumb and green witch before you.

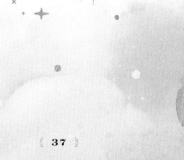

SPELL FOR A PROTECTIVE WREATH

Made from natural materials, such as herbs, twigs, flowers, and other elements, wreaths have served many purposes throughout the ages. Unending circles, they symbolize eternity and the cycle of the seasons. In the spring, pay attention to what blooms first and what green returns to your natural spaces. To welcome spring, incorporate the fresh energy of these vibrant new plants into your wreath. A wreath hanging on a door can provide magical protection for the home.

To refresh and boost the energies you'd like to raise, customize your wreath to your intentions and take advantage of materials such as herbs in your garden or local seasonal blooms.

To weave a protective spell, use these shielding herbs to dress and guard your home with the energies of the season:

ᒋ angelica	ᒋ fern	ᒋ rosemary
ᒋ basil	ᒋ foxglove	ᒋ rowan
ᒋ bay laurel	ᒋ holly	ᒋ sage
ᒋ chives	ᒋ mugwort	ᒋ star anise
ᒋ dill	ᒋ oregano	ᒋ witch hazel

When you hang your wreath, cast a circle of protection on your home by speaking aloud over it. You can create your own charm that feels right or use this one:

I cast this circle on my door
with herbs so rich and deep in lore
that from all ills protected be
my home will ne'er be harmed nor poor.

After you hang your wreath, reflect on how gathering the materials for it helped you connect to the season. What new plants or natural allies did you encounter? What did you see, hear, smell, touch, or taste that made you feel connected to the natural world?

What intentions are you bringing to your home by hanging this wreath in your space? Explain what shift in energy you hope to bring. How will you honor those intentions with your actions this spring?

SPELL FOR SETTING INTENTIONS WITH PLANTS

For all your magical work, you need no special tools other than the herbs, a mindful presence, and a focus on setting intentions in tune with the natural rhythms around you. Setting those intentions guides your magical journey, but your intuition also helps show the way. Many refer to intuition metaphorically as their "gut," and learning to trust yours is an important skill in your magical work. You not only will gain insights into the world around you, but you also will sense when your magic is working or perhaps needs a boost, such as with the herbs here. If your intuition is warning you that something doesn't feel right, take heed. It's usually right. It's one of the best tools in your magical bag, and your herbal allies will support it.

When working to achieve a goal, the process sometimes can stretch ahead for what feels like miles. Keep your intentions front of mind and don't lose sight of what you're tending. A little herbal spell can help you keep your eyes on the prize, whatever that may be. Gather the following elements:

- clean pot of a size appropriate for your space
- glass of water
- organic potting soil
- paper and pen
- seeds or seedlings for calendula, nasturtium, sunflower, or another edible flower. (If you're feeling ambitious, try a vegetable seed or seedling.)

Fill the pot ³/₄ full of soil and pat it down firmly. Write your goal(s) on the piece of paper. Roll or fold the paper as small as you can and insert it, like planting a seed, in the center of the pot. Following the provided instructions, place the seed or seedling in the center of the pot, atop your paper, and cover with soil. Pat the topsoil firmly in place. Place the pot in a spot where you will see it every day and where it will receive the appropriate amount of sunlight. Water until the soil feels damp but not flooded. Place a glass of water next to it to encourage you to remember to water it. As the seed grows, reflect on how the goals you have planted also are growing.

This winter, when you were setting goals or making resolutions, what plans did you make for spring? Have you planted those seeds and begun acting on those goals? How can you tend to those aspirations today and in the immediate future?

What plant did you first grow or tend? Did you try growing seedlings in elementary school or help in a family garden? What was your first houseplant? What did those plants teach you that you still carry with you? Reflect on what you enjoyed about them. What knowledge that you have now would have been helpful then?

SPELL FOR IDENTIFYING YOUR ROLE

All herbs come from the earth and therefore carry its energies and wisdom, but each herb has unique properties and spirit, exhibiting different qualities and uses. In that way, all herbs are magical, but what makes any particular herb magical can differ for every person.

An herb's shape, color, or fragrance can convey or invoke particular narratives or meaning. Its relationship with animals or sacred status among indigenous peoples can imbue special standing to specific herbs. When using herbs in rituals and remedies, the observance of cause and effect can lead to lessons passing from generation to generation. All of these elements contribute to a plant's otherworldly properties, and the magic lies in all its parts: roots, stems, bark, leaves, flowers, fruit, and seeds.

Early witches, who plied their herbal craft with magic spells and spirit guides, were usually just natural healers, wise women valued and consulted for remedies and advice yet also misunderstood. Today's herbal magic devotees use their herbal wisdom to promote peace, tolerance, balance, living in harmony with nature, and honoring the earth for her gifts.

You probably can trace some piece of ancestral lore, as familiar as a grandparent's special dish, to an herb and its magic. Are you a healer, helper, creator, or sustainer? Do you charge ahead to lead or provide necessary support to help someone else cross the finish line? To help you find your role, this meditation spell will connect you with your own narrative.

You'll need a quiet space and a timer—on your phone, a kitchen appliance, or a free-standing one—to help you contain your meditation time. If you like, you can hold a favorite herb or scent your space with a favorite essential oil to help focus your mind. Set your timer for 15–20 minutes, a good chunk of time to sit in stillness undisturbed and long enough to create a space outside the normal flow of your day.

Breathe deeply and gently through your nose. Consider your favorite plant and your relationship to it. Envision each leaf, how the branches divide, the tone of its colors, and its scent. Picture holding it in your hand and imagine where it grows in your home or in nature. Once you've centered the plant in your mind, focus on what you know about the plant in relation to you. What are its role in its ecosystem and its uses for people? Where does it grow in the wild, and how did it come to you? What part does it play in your life? How do you support each other? Do you see this plant as a partner, pet, or producer? Consider the narrative that exists between you and this plant. Use the insights you glean to shape your relationship to all of your plants, expanding, developing, and changing as feels right.

If you could put a name to your role and relationship with your favorite plant, how would you describe it? Does this role bring you joy, or would you change something about it? Does it reflect your larger relationship to the natural world? How so?

SPELL FOR EMBRACING PLANT WISDOM

Defining plant intelligence can prove tricky, and researchers have tried to measure it based on sensory abilities, movement, memory, adaptability, and communication systems—all points that allow people to argue for and against a plant's ability to possess and demonstrate intelligence. Skeptics often dismiss the notion because of the plant kingdom's slow pace and the seemingly invisible nature of its responses, but that slowness can serve plants' abilities to adapt to their environments and continue to grow and reproduce.

Scientists are beginning to understand that plants do have intelligence and an ability to learn, remember, communicate, and cooperate. In a forest, trees exchange nutrients and information about threats via an underground network of roots and fungi, for example. Above ground, plants communicate using chemicals and scents to warn of danger, deter predators, and invite pollinators. Studies have shown that plants respond to sound—that is, vibrations—as well, specifically frequencies between 125 and 250 Hz, which happen to be the average frequencies for male and female voices, respectively.

It has a reputation, but talking to your plants does seem to help them grow. A Royal Horticultural Society study showed that plants, when spoken to over a period of time, grew more vigorously than those ignored. So among the vibrations of your aura, thoughts, voice, and movements, your plants do look forward to your visits. If you listen carefully, they may share their secrets with you as well.

The best spell to honor the intelligence of plants is cultivating a sense of them as individuals. This spell takes some time; it's not a one-and-done charm.

Choose a single plant, one you're tending already, one you purchase for this purpose, or even your first seedling. Place a small notebook and pen next to it. At the same time each day, for two weeks, write a few notes about what you observe about this specific plant. Pay attention to the color of its leaves and the progress of its growth, to how it reacts to the light and weather. Spend at least a few minutes with it each day.

What messages is the plant communicating to you through its growth, behavior, and responses to your attention and care?

If you could speak to it, what would you tell this plant? If you could hear it respond plainly, how would it reply?

....

....

....

....

....

....

....

....

....

....

....

....

....

....

....

SPELL FOR SPEAKING WITH FLOWERS

Called nosegays or posies starting in the 1400s, small bouquets of herbs and flowers offer protection to wearers. Over the centuries, they developed into a secret messaging system, based on the plants' assigned meanings. The concept of the language of flowers reached its height in popularity during the Victorian era, when the bouquets, largely decorative, were called tussie-mussies. Numerous books have decoded and detailed this language, called floriography. The complex meanings contain many nuances. For example, bay leaf signifies glory, motherwort hints at concealed love, and saffron warns of excess.

Whether tucked into a wreath, gathered in a vase, bundled to hang, or scattered about, herbs and flowers have powerful natural charms that can help you direct energies and outcomes in your home. Their beauty and scent carry messages of luck, love, fertility, and healing and offer silent reminders of the intentions you seek to manifest.

As a spell to speak with flowers, fashion your own floral "letter" to yourself. Create a bouquet to unlock your heart and soothe your soul with gentleness. Use floral messengers to create a custom spell to say exactly what you need to hear. These floriographic meanings will get you started:

ENCOURAGEMENT
delphinium

FAMILY HARMONY AND LOVE
apple blossom, basil, bleeding heart, gardenia, sweet alyssum

FERTILITY
acorn, carrot, fig, geranium,
pine, sunflower

LUCK AND MONEY
acorn, basil, bluebell, buckeye,
daffodil, honeysuckle, moss,
nutmeg, pine, poppy

FRIENDSHIP
lemon, sweet pea

NEW VENTURES
bay laurel, mint, myrtle, tansy

HEALING
angelica, bay leaf, fennel, ivy,
lemon balm, marigold

PROTECTION
cactus, dill, fennel, lilac, peony,
rosemary, witch hazel

REMEMBRANCE
fennel, lavender, pansy, rosemary

SUCCESS
bay leaf, jasmine, strawberry

ROMANTIC LOVE
carnation, daisy, lavender, lemon
verbena, pansy, peppermint, rose,
rosemary

WISDOM
iris, sage, sunflower

SLEEP
chamomile, hyacinth, lavender,
thyme

As you gather the herbs and blooms that carry your intentions forward, thank them for their gifts. They may remain silent, but they are potent, lending their energies to your wishes. As you arrange them in whatever fashion you desire, kindly ask for their help, as you need it. Display the bouquet in a prominent place where its message can resonate in your space.

What message do you want this bouquet to carry and project in your home and why?

If you were to build a bouquet message for someone else who could understand it only intuitively, without a written guide, who is the person, what would you put in it, and what would you hope to communicate?

SPELL FOR BOOSTING YOUR POWERS WITH THE PLANETS

Born from the Earth, nurtured by the Sun, and cooled under the Moon, herbs carry powerful energies that define their magical properties. When you combine your energies with their magic, their true power comes into being. As you learn about each herb's individual magic and wisdom, you need only a few spells and rituals to get you on your magical way. But to heighten your magical workings, you can layer other systems of energy with an herb's. In addition to energies carried in its environment, shape, color, scent, and even the unexplainable, it has correspondences with other entities that amplify its energy.

The planetary correspondences here connect to astrology. When you want to embrace the specific energy of a planet, use herbs that connect to it. Alternatively, you can supercharge herbs by heeding when and where the planets become most active in astrology.

PLANETARY COMPANIONS

Just as you can see the influence of the Moon's phases on Earth's tides or the Sun's ability to evaporate rain and initiate growth, each herb has a classical planetary companion that lends its powerful status and wisdom to the herb's own power. Use these corollaries to guide your garden work and call on the power of these heavenly bodies as an active spell to encourage your spirit and your garden to thrive in balance.

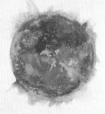

SUN: The warmth of the Sun represents growth, prosperity, and protection. Herbs, plants, and flowers associated with the Sun can combine for money spells, creativity rituals, and centering work.

Herbs: cedar, chamomile, cloves, frankincense, sunflower

MERCURY: Call on Mercury to influence areas of study, travel—worldly and otherworldly—and business. Use its associated herbs, plants, and flowers when communication is key, new skills are required, or a business venture needs guidance. But beware its flashiness. Beauty, while glamorous, is fleeting.

Herbs: chervil, cinnamon, fennel, lavender, mugwort, poppy, rosemary

VENUS: The plants, flowers, and herbs corresponding to Venus embody her attributes of love, lushness, and beauty. Call on these showy and fragrant plants in all matters of love, pleasure, and the arts.

Herbs: birch, jasmine, lavender, rose, rosemary, sage, verbena, violet

MOON: The all-seeing gaze of the Moon imbues the plants associated with it. Qualities enhanced by this association include interpreting dreams and divining the future. These plants refresh and rejuvenate the body, soul, and spirit much like a dip into cool water on a hot day. Use these unique powers when fertility, intuition, emotions, or the subconscious are involved.

Herbs: gardenia, jasmine, moonwort, myrtle, poppy, verbena, white rose

MARS: The energy of Mars and its plants protects and defends, builds strength and courage, and burns with passion and masculine energy. Incorporate herbs, plants, and flowers under Mars's tutelage when your inner warrior feels sidelined or daily conflict has you in knots.

Herbs: carnation, nettle, patchouli, pepper, pine, red rose

JUPITER: This beneficent ruler wishes for those under its protection to flourish. Though a potentate, Jupiter is nurturing and generous. Harness its influence when matters of authority, faith, and the legal realm are at play. Jupiter's spell also channels contentment.

Herbs: beech, cedar, garlic, hawthorn, leek, nutmeg, oak, thistle

SATURN: Use Saturn's energies to define limits and set boundaries—in the sense of being realistic and self-protective, not punishing. Plants influenced by Saturn grow in places that other plants won't thrive, such as in shade or poor soil. Invoke the energy of Saturn when you need to kick a bad habit, remove a negative influence from your orbit, or remember that tough times can produce beautiful results.

Herbs: basil, hemlock, hyacinth, juniper, moss, nettle, peppermint, thyme

Identify your favorite two or three herbs. Which planet or planets have traditional associations with them? What patterns do you detect in your preferences and energies?

SPELL FOR CONNECTING TO CYCLES

One of the most important aspects of creating an herbal garden is tuning into the natural rhythms and cycles of tending. Use astrological periods as containers for specific tasks in your garden and herbal work. For example, in the Northern Hemisphere, Aries aligns with the impatient season of seed starting, Taurus with nurturing tender seedlings, Gemini with the busy thinning of vigorous growth, and so on. Where you live, the seasons and star cycles might not align precisely, but look for seasonal tasks that embrace the energy of the zodiac.

ZODIAC SIGNS

Each sign of the zodiac has a reputation for certain traits—some good, some not always charming—embodied by those born under its influence. Knowing your sign and the signs of those you love, along with each sign's associated traits, can help you mix and match herbs to direct your magic energies toward the positive and away from the negative.

ARIES THE RAM
(March 21–April 20)

FIRE SIGN

Herbs: basil, chervil, geranium, nettle

Aries plants are spicy and red, like the planet. Their energies amplify courage, determination, and confidence, which may help counter impatience, moodiness, and aggressiveness.

GEMINI THE TWINS
(May 22–June 21)

AIR SIGN

Herbs: anise, dill, lavender, parsley

Gemini plants invite calm. They feel friendly, gentle, charming, adaptable, and sometimes curious. Call on Gemini energies to counter nervousness, inconsistency, and indecision.

TAURUS THE BULL
(April 21–May 21)

EARTH SIGN

Herbs: marsh mallow, thyme, violet

Taurus plants are sweet-scented and lovely. Their energies amplify reliability, patience, and practicality, which may help counter stubbornness, possessiveness, and a bullish attitude.

CANCER THE CRAB
(June 22–July 22)

WATER SIGN

Herbs: aloe, bay leaf, lemon balm, sage

Cancer's plants encourage nurturing, bravery, and loyalty, which can help counter moodiness, defensiveness, and insecurity.

LEO THE LION
(July 23–August 22)

FIRE SIGN

Herbs: chamomile, lemon balm, sunflower

Leo's plants are large, bright, and uplifting. Incorporate their spiritual messages to invoke pride, creativity, and warm-heartedness and counter arrogance, stubbornness, or inflexibility.

LIBRA THE SCALES
(September 24–October 23)

AIR SIGN

Herbs: bergamot, elderberry, thyme

Libra's plants are handsome. Their energies encourage cooperation, fair-mindedness, and graciousness and can counter indecision and frivolity.

VIRGO THE MAIDEN
(August 23–September 23)

EARTH SIGN

Herbs: caraway, dill, marjoram, mint

Virgo's plants have a definitive, clearly outlined shape. Use Virgo's energies to enhance analysis, insight, and productivity, as well as loyalty and kindness, and to counter critical, anxious, or unhappy energies.

SCORPIO THE SCORPION
(October 24–November 22)

WATER SIGN

Herbs: basil, coriander, nettle, sage

Scorpio's plants are hearty, persistent, and a little thorny. They speak of passion, bravery, and resiliency, and their energies can counter jealously, secrecy, and emotional instability.

SAGITTARIUS
THE ARCHER

(November 23–December 21)

FIRE SIGN

Herbs: basil, borage, chervil, saffron, sage

Sagittarius plants are large and important. Their energies support adventurousness, generosity, intelligence, and positivity and can help counter impatience, rudeness, and the tendency to overpromise.

AQUARIUS
THE WATER BEARER

(January 21–February 19)

AIR SIGN

Herbs: fennel, rosemary, violet

Aquarius plants proudly display their individuality and grow in unexpected places. Their innate ability to calm and inspire can boost generosity, humanity, tolerance, and perceptiveness and counter moodiness, an inability to compromise, and aloofness.

CAPRICORN THE GOAT

(December 22–January 20)

EARTH SIGN

Herbs: caraway, rosemary, tarragon

Capricorn's plants are sturdy and resilient. Their energies can support discipline, leadership, and analytical thinking and counter selfishness, condescension, and a tendency not to listen to others.

PISCES THE FISH

(February 20–March 20)

WATER SIGN

Herbs: basil, borage, lemon balm, sage

Pisces plants have an association with water. Their energies promote health, artistic creativity, compassion, and intuition and counter worry, indecision, and a tendency to be overly trusting.

To activate the energy of a particular sign, prepare a spell sachet or small spell bottle that contains the herbs associated with the sign you want to invoke, then place the vessel in the space in which you want to focus this energy. For example, create a Gemini spell bottle to keep on your desk or an Aries sachet for your gym bag. Bring Capricorn energy to your job interview and a mix of Scorpio, Pisces, and Cancer, all water signs, to therapy.

What seasonal or herbal tasks align with your astrological energies?
Consult your star chart and see how your favorite herbs correspond
to important placements in it. Note them below. How can you harness
those energies to help your herbal allies thrive where you live?

SPELL TO BUILD ROUTINE

A solid routine ensures that you have time to tend to yourself, your garden, and all your obligations without rush or stress. The garden has its own routines, flowers closing as the sun sets and leaves unfurling in the warmth of spring. If you decide to grow plants, you must care for them regularly, whether that entails deadheading spent flowers or ensuring that each plant has enough water to thrive.

Just as the planets correspond to specific energies, so the days of the week resonate with specific tasks. You can use magic to inform your routines and help you achieve a manageable, supportive rhythm. Bringing a bit of astrology into your practice offers a great way to further sync your routine to the skies. The days of the week take their names from deities associated with heavenly bodies, so crafting a spell, ritual, or prayer on a particular day triples the energetic influence of the herbs used: planetary influence + daily influence + herbal energy.

MONDAY FOR THE MOON

Herbs: gardenia, jasmine, moonwort, myrtle, poppy, verbena, white rose
Monday's lunar tendencies give you time to reconnect and work with your emotional depths, including:

- clairvoyance
- cleansing
- dreams
- emotional healing
- family
- guidance
- intuition
- peace
- truth

TUESDAY FOR MARS

Herbs: carnation, nettle, patchouli, pepper, pine, red rose
Honor your inner warrior and channel Mars's energy in your herbal work when you seek:

- bravery
- courage
- energy
- love
- passion
- power
- protection

WEDNESDAY FOR MERCURY

Herbs: chervil, cinnamon, fennel, lavender, mugwort, poppy, rosemary
Send your missives into the universe on the wings of messenger
Mercury when working your herbal magic for:

- charisma
- communication
- creativity
- spiritual awareness
- travel
- wisdom

THURSDAY FOR JUPITER

Herbs: beech, cedar, garlic, hawthorn, leek, nutmeg, oak, thistle
The sky's the limit with Jupiter on your side. Its power can boost your
herbal energies when pursuing:

- career
- generosity
- luck
- patience
- peace
- sincerity
- wealth

FRIDAY FOR VENUS

Herbs: birch, jasmine, lavender, rose, rosemary, sage, verbena, violet
Born from the sea and destined to love both gods and mortals, Venus
days can help you cultivate:

- abundance
- affection
- beauty
- fertility
- forgiveness
- friendship
- good luck
- harmony
- love
- money
- peace
- renewal
- romance
- success

SATURDAY FOR SATURN

Herbs: basil, hemlock, hyacinth, juniper, moss, nettle, peppermint, thyme
With its deep connection to agriculture, Saturn's healing energies can guide you in matters of:

- grounding
- home
- justice
- letting go
- peace
- protection from negative energy

SUNDAY FOR THE SUN

Herbs: cedar, chamomile, cloves, frankincense, sunflower
Set a positive tone for what lies ahead. Take advantage of solar energies related to:

- confidence
- creativity
- energy
- healing
- hope
- intuition
- joy
- mental clarity
- peace
- protection
- spirituality
- strength
- wealth

To anchor yourself in your routine with a spell, create rituals that incorporate herbalism into your daily life. Use the above guide to create your own meaningful schedule that activates the energy of each day in the morning. On Monday, for example, wear a jasmine perfume. Include pepper in your Tuesday breakfast. Each a cinnamon oat bowl on Wednesday. On Thursday, use a cedar bodywash in your bath or shower. Deploy your most fragrant lotion on Friday. Treat yourself to a cup of peppermint tea on Saturday, and snack on some sunflower seeds on Sunday.

How does your ideal schedule look? Does it correspond to these planetary planning tools, or do you have other guidelines for your week? Write out your current schedule and your ideal schedule and consider how you can change your days to bring them closer to ideal, especially finding more time to connect to nature, rest, and practice self-care.

SPELL FOR INVITING MAGIC INTO YOUR GARDEN

As with all forms of magic, you need reverence and respect for Mother Earth. To attune yourself to her energy cycles, you should try to grow your own herbs, plants, or flowers. Selecting, nurturing, and harvesting your own plants pull you along with the flow of the seasons and connect you to the elements. Gardening physically connects you to the energies of the earth—the warmth of the soil, the fragrance of the herbs, the sound of the wind, and the feel of the rain—and plugs you into the harmony of nature. Even one special herb on a sunny windowsill can prove enchanting and uplifting.

That said, it's not always practical or possible to grow your own herbs. Your innate magic amplifies herbs' magic, releasing their energies and messages into the Universe. If your herbs come from a more practical source—say, a local grocery store or farmers' market—they will serve just as powerfully in your spells. The key to a magical life is the ability to set intentions to form the basis of communicating with universal energies and to believe in the power of your actions to influence and amplify the good in all.

Your garden represents its own spell come to life. To encourage specific types of energy and to cast place-based spells to enchant your life, plant the spell you'd like to cast on the world around you. To start, select the plants that communicate your desires and intentions. You can start with a single selection—maybe sweetpeas to cut and share to celebrate a friendship—or a combination as complex as your favorite spell jar, with pansies, myrtle, lilac, and bluebells to create a home of good memories and abundance.

When you plan your plants, keep a list of what you've planted and why. Press the flowers or weave them into a wreath to pull the blessings of the space you've created into your home year round. Treat this planting plan like an altar and watch both the garden and its energy flourish around you.

What herbal magic already forms part of your routine? This might take place in your kitchen, drinking tea, or plant care. What more explicitly magical practices—such as building altars, burning incense, or other rituals—can you incorporate into your routine that might connect you to your herbal practice in new ways?

SUMMER

epending on where you live and work with plants, this time of abundance and outdoor enjoyment also may become a time of hard work or slowing down, depending on the fierceness of the sun and the variety of plant-tending tasks available. Plants usually require more water and attention now, but they also will reward you with lush color and fragrance.

This generous season, full of blooms and fruit, constantly changes from day to day, week to week. Dig deep and partake in all the juicy joys of its sweet, luxurious bounty. Trim your herbal plants to dry in big bunches and save a taste of summer for the deep of winter. In this season, growth and plenty will reward the work you invest in cutting back your herbal allies.

Summer calls for attentive maintenance of all your garden spaces. Trellised, trimmed, and tied, most plants need a bit of structure and support to reach their full potential. We humans are much the same, and the following spells and prompts will help you structure your own growth to ensure that you invest all that time and energy into blooming as beautifully and resiliently as possible.

A Guide to Growing & Harvesting

TRIM TO GROW

Plants need tending as much as people do, and sometimes that means trimming them back. Depending on the appropriate season, they have a time for growth and a time for dying back. Many fruiting plants, such as raspberries or grapes, fruit only on new growth or, as with rosemary or lavender, will need a heavy pruning after winter to thrive in the summer.

DEADHEAD FOR MORE BLOOMS

It may seem like a shame to remove beautiful blooms from plants while they thrive, but flowers become seed heads. If you don't take them off the plant, it will put all its energy into seeds . . . and no new flowers! If you want blooms all season, remove fading blooms quickly. If you grow them to display, trim them for your home with zero guilt or reservation.

KNOW WHEN A PLANT'S TIME HAS PASSED

Some annual plants simply can't grow beyond their season. Radishes and greens might bolt if temperatures spike or drought alights. Peas and parsleys wilt under intense heat, and your tomatoes simply won't fruit after a certain point. Be judicious about removing plants past their prime and replacing them with more appropriate planting that anticipates the turning of the season.

COPE WITH ABUNDANCE OR SCARCITY

The height of the season in a successful garden can feel a little overwhelming or disappointing, depending on how it goes. You will do your best, but especially with outdoor gardening, you are relying on the sun and rain. If you wind up with an abundance, cut things back and preserve the herbs by drying, pickling, or preserving. When in doubt, give them to family, friends, or neighbors. If the opposite occurs, give yourself permission to buy new plants, try new things, and release perfection in favor of learning and growing your skills.

FIND SEASONAL USES FOR EATING AND TREATING

Investigate unconventional uses for your garden treasures and explore the fascinating world of preservation. Drying and freezing offer useful, approachable entry points to keeping plant matter usable beyond its season, but you needn't stick just to those two methods. Try your hand at pickling and making cordials, jams, syrups, and tinctures—anything to harvest the maximum from your bounty.

SPELL FOR CLARIFYING INTENTIONS

Action springs from intention, and intentions should come from the seeds of gratitude. Everything consists of energy, and all energy vibrates at different intensities. So, too, do your intentions. The universal nature of energy means that all things connect, and energies, like ripples in a pond, expand outward. Clearly formulating your energy-filled intentions and releasing them into the Universe allow the energy to come back to you multiplied.

Setting your intentions with spellwork formalizes the reflections that drive them and the actions you'll need to embody them. To begin, define your intentions: What do you need? What do you seek? What do you wish? What needs attention in your life? Reach deep into your soul to acknowledge, without fear or judgment, what matters to you and what will make you truly happy. Setting specific intentions based on these self-defined priorities leads to goals aligned with your values and dreams. Defining your intentions keeps you focused and living mindfully in the present and can help improve your overall well-being. Important, too, are living mindfully without judgment, learning to accept what is, and working to change circumstances as desired.

Reaping the bounty of a beautifully tended garden means planning, planting, and weeding, an apt description of intention-setting in action. Inhale the magical scents of your herbs and prepare to watch your intentions bloom. Vibrational energy ripples created when you release your intentions into the Universe cause chain reactions that can take time to reveal themselves. Results may be delayed or not what you expected, but they likely are there if you look and listen carefully.

For an easy way to set intentions into action as a spell, write them on a piece of paper in the most detailed and specific way that you can. Take your time; the more specific you are, the more the Universe can help you. Consider the steps involved in supporting those intentions and include those as well. Bury this letter in your garden to plant the seeds of your intentions. Then plant a favorite plant above it to mark the space and use the blooming period to reflect on your progress.

If you feel your intentions are falling on fallow ground, remember these tips:

- **Be clear.** Identify what lies in your heart. Clarify your signals.

- **Be consistent.** Focus on what's important.

- **Be attuned.** Review your timing and assess your energy levels.

- **Be patient.** Magic, like Mother Nature, won't be hurried.

- **Be present.** Cultivate gratitude as you work toward your goals.

- **Be kind.** Herbal magic requires a special relationship with the earth. Be respectful to all living things.

- **Believe.** Tend to your gifts and let the magic within you bloom and spread.

Use the space below to identify parts of your life about which you'd like to be more intentional. How can you set specific, clear intentions about what you want or need to change? Select one option and cast that as your first intention-setting spell.

SPELL FOR GROUNDING YOURSELF

Time in nature eases stress, increases focus, boosts creativity, and promotes empathy—all valuable results. Adding meditation to enhance your herbal magic offers another tool to access your inner thoughts and feelings, which can become intentions set and energy released to achieve goals. Mindful meditation is the practice of being present in the moment, without judgment, and paying attention to your body: breathing, sensations, emotions, and thoughts. Meditation doesn't have to tune everything out. It also can tune you in to the present and yourself. As with all new habits, mindful meditation takes practice and consistency. Even just five minutes a day can help. Once you feel its benefits in your life, you will crave the quiet peace that meditation affords.

When you're ready, follow this guided meditation.

Find a quiet, comfortable place. To connect with natural energies, ideal for boosting mood and peacefulness, go outside if possible. If you want or need to time your session, set a gentle alarm now.

Close your eyes. Limit visual distractions if you feel comfortable doing so.

Breathe. Bring your attention to your breath. Breathe naturally. Feel your body grow on the in-breath and collapse on the out-breath.

Inhale. Focus on the scent around you, filling you from top to bottom, cleansing and clearing any negativity, hurt, or fear. If indoors, focus on the scent of a candle or incense.

Visualize. Exhaling releases all stress and discomfort from your body as you replace it by inhaling soothing kindness.

Focus. Keep your attention on your breathing. If your attention wanders, gently acknowledge it and return focus to your breath.

Be grateful. When you're ready or your timer sounds, return to your surroundings. Open your eyes. Wiggle your toes. Place your hands on the ground, floor, or chair where you're sitting. Give thanks for the quiet time and the welcoming space before returning to your normal activities.

What smells and sounds do you notice more during meditation? What about them makes them more noticeable? What draws you toward them?

Where else would you like to try meditating to stimulate these senses and ground you? How do you think each location will affect you differently?

SPELL FOR CONNECTING TO THE PRESENT

Bring your meditation to a natural space you know well, be it a safe and comfortable wild space, your garden, or even just an open window. Using the grounding meditation, focus specifically on the natural elements around you. If you feel particularly centered in the moment while focusing on scent and sound, open your eyes for observational meditation. Keep your focus on the space and moment you are occupying, gently setting aside any concerns, stress, or errant thoughts. Afterward, record the experience in a meditation or reflection journal.

For a more advanced practice, repeat the meditation over the course of a month or season. Record your observations, focusing on the plants and environment as they are in each moment. Heed the blooming of the flowers, the sounds of birds, the feel of the breeze or the sun. Include as many sensory details as you can.

After meditation and observation, how have your senses sharpened? What new details about this familiar space have revealed themselves to you?

SPELL FOR CAPTURING INTENTION

Some people turn spell jars, classic containers for capturing intention and magical motivation, into herbal charm bags or herbal prayer bottles. Only the intentionality in assembling the parts for a magical end matters, so choose a vessel that makes the most sense for your materials and intended place of use. A clear glass container lets you see the layers of the magical intentions you've set as a reminder of your magic at work and the specific goal of your spells.

Anything you can imagine can fill an herbal spell jar: a wish for a bountiful garden, financial success, romantic love, family harmony, spiritual healing, good luck, home protection, increased fertility, self-love, peace for the world—you name it. But remember, your herbal magic must do no harm, so good works only. Some of the best magical outcomes occur when practiced for yourself, but herbal spell jars can make lovely gifts for family and friends to help boost specific energies in their lives, where—as they may have requested or you may have noticed—they need a helping hand.

A spell jar simply incubates your magic. Creating an herbal one is simple:

1. Create your intention and focus on the energy you wish to invoke.

2. Select a vessel. In the spirit of green living, repurpose something you already have, such as a glass food jar that once held baby food, jam, mayonnaise, sauce, spice, or yogurt. The size you choose depends only on the size of your wish or intention.

3. Select the natural items that vibrate with a corresponding energy to convey your message and further your intentions. Consider your earlier experiences with astrological resonances (page 61) and floriography (page 50) to convey meaning and intention.

4. Cleanse the jar and natural items for your spell. A moon bath (setting the items under a full moon) offers the simplest and most powerful choice. A water bath, if the items are water-friendly, or an herbal smudging can do the job, too, as can offering a simple prayer to thank them for their previous work and to cleanse the energies for a new purpose.

5. Infuse your jar and its new contents with your intentions. If you can, on a safe surface, light a candle in a color corresponding to your intentions. Sit quietly for a moment, holding the items, reflecting on your intention, setting it in your mind, imprinting it in your heart, and infusing it into the magical charms. Thank them for the work they are about to do.

6. Build your herbal spell jar. As you fill the jar, place the heaviest components on the bottom, such as Himalayan salt, clean soil, nutmeg seeds, acorns, seashells, crystals, or coins. Place medium-weight items—dried rose buds, dried lavender blossoms, bark, buttons, paper—in the middle. Finally, place lightest items on top, including dried flower buds, dried herbs, feathers, and so on. To prevent mold or other unwanted growth that can occur with items containing water, use only dry or dried items. If you feel an aromatic boost will help, sprinkle a bit of essential oil into the jar.

7. As you fill your jar, speak your intentions aloud, ideally something specific to your chosen outcome. The words don't need to feel like a *spell*. They just need to be specific and clear about your goal.

8. Seal the jar. If the candle is still burning and the top of the jar is flat and stable enough, place the candle on the jar and let it burn down as you meditate on your wish.

9. Place the sealed jar on your altar or in an area of your home corresponding to your intention. Alternately, if you are able and you wish, bury it or place it in a closet if you're working to banish something from your life and need your magic to work on its own away from you.

Imagine a spell jar for an intention or goal you have right now. What would you put into it, in what order, and why? What would each element placed inside mean for you?

SPELL FOR BANISHING BURDENS

You may associate roses with love, but they have enormous power to heal as well, especially when burdens weigh heavily on your mind and spirit. Don't let the ubiquity of roses, a common but powerful ally, deter you from using them in your practice. But if any spell calls for you to consume or apply the roses topically, use petals from roses you've grown, foraged away from roadsides, or purchased from a reputable herbalist. Commercial growers treat roses heavily with chemicals, so you never should use them in teas, masks, or baths.

For this ritual, gather as many rose petals as you can from your garden or from a grocer or farmers' market, along with a large bowl of water, a green candle, a heatproof container for the candle, and matches. In a quiet, outdoor area without disturbances—near a body of water, small or large (in which case, omit the bowl of water)—lay a circle of petals near the water, reserving 5 to 10 petals. If you aren't near water, place the bowl of water in the center of the circle along with the candle and reserved petals.

Step into the circle with gratitude for the opportunity to learn from your pain. Take a moment to set your intention to release your burdens and to open yourself to healing. When ready, light the candle with a match and sit next to the water. Pick up a petal, one at a time. Hold it in your hand and appreciate its soothing feel and scent. Visualize it absorbing the struggle you wish to release. When ready to release the encumbrance, float the petal in the water, watching it drift away from you. Repeat with the remaining petals, infusing each with a different burden or, if particularly weighty, different elements of the same burden.

When all the petals are floating in the water, carrying your struggle away, visualize your pain moving out of sight. When it has gone, extinguish the candle, empty the bowl (if used) to nurture the Earth, and leave the remaining petals as a thank you to nature.

What are you holding that makes you feel bad about who you haven't been or who you are now and why? How can you untangle those feelings from your joys and then minimize them?

If you could shed parts of yourself to start over, what would you discard and what would you become? What's stopping you from doing so now?

SPELL FOR WORKING WITH THE NEW MOON

For millennia, the moon's mystical light and cyclical phases have
guided people worldwide in all aspects of daily life. All who heed her
charms worship, revere, bless, and learn from this lovely orb. It takes
about twenty-nine days for the moon to pass through all eight phases,
from new moon to full moon and back again. Those phases offer a cycle
of light and dark: bright light to see clearly, spark energy, and celebrate;
darkness for rest, quiet, and contemplation, to learn from mistakes
and correct course. Understanding the energies and rhythms of these
phases offers you yet another way to harness the natural energies of
the universe to help communicate and bring about your intentions.
Use the waxing (growing) and waning (diminishing) energies of the
moon's phases to set, implement, evaluate, revise, achieve, celebrate,
and assess your intention-filled life. Coordinating your herbal allies,
thoughts, dreams, and plans with the moon's natural cycle can help
you achieve all you desire. Nurture, tend, and grow your dreams as the
phases unfold. The magic is there for the taking.

Pairing herbs with the Moon's energetic phases can add powerful
influences to your magic. Incorporating herbs not only for their innate
energies and unique powers but also ones cultivated or blessed by the
moon's gaze will help you engage more powerfully in herbal magic.
So search the skies for a bit of cosmic correspondence and remember
that even the smallest signs can bear great meaning. As with all magic,
time, patience, and practice will unlock the results you desire. For a new
beginning, the New Moon is like tilling soil to unlock its fertile potential.
It's the perfect time to turn over the soil of your mind and pull the weeds
of what isn't serving you. Assess what you need to put forth a rich
harvest. Make space for what's new and fresh.

For a gentle and welcoming new moon spell, gather dried herbs, a candle, paper, pen, and fireproof dish. Select herbs for specific intentionalities, such as rosemary for clarity and remembrance, sage for clearing and opening space, or cloves for protection and manifestation, and burn them safely, using their smoke to cleanse your spellwork space. Light the candle and write your intentions on a slip of paper. Touch a corner of the paper to the flame and place it safely in the dish. Allow the paper to burn completely and dispose of the ashes where they can contribute to the growth of a plant or garden. As the plants draw from the soil containing the ashes, they'll take up your intentions with them.

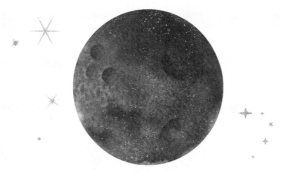

The fertile Earth has given birth to each and every herb.

With powers ripe to stir new life—each bloom, each leaf, and seed—

within the Earth to bloom again as much as within me.

O' Moon and goddess, do unite to grant my wish indeed.

In preparation for the prior spell, do this exercise on the new moon as well if possible. What are you looking to create in your life? What ventures do you want to infuse with fresh commitment and energy and why? Bring these intentions to your New Moon spell.

SPELL FOR WORKING WITH THE WAXING MOON

While the New and Full Moons tend to receive more attention for spellwork, they're not the only times to make magic under the Moon. The complete cycle has plenty of space for all intentions; it's about finding the right time for your schedule and the intentions that you're cultivating. If you're looking to grow a new habit or goal, consider using the waxing cycle to accumulate that energy as the Moon grows in the sky.

WAXING CRESCENT

Growing light awakens intentions. The energies of this phase stir activity. Set your intentions and plant their seeds to sprout. Channel the growing energy of the moon and apply it to your intentions.

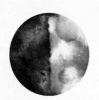

FIRST QUARTER MOON

Stronger vibrations sharpen intentions and intuition. Allow the moon to stir your energies, taking root to grow full and strong. Push forward toward establishing new patterns and draw perseverance toward your goals.

WAXING GIBBOUS

Increasing energy spurs action. In the moon's growing light, celebrate new growth and positive change as your intentions, like your growing herbs, show their promise and reward your hard work.

To work with the increasing energy and fulfillment of the waxing moon, fill a sachet of the following herbs and keep it with you: laurel for victory, lavender for calm and protection, and nettle for nourishment. This small sachet works as a walking spell, a way of carrying the energy of a spell with you. You can tuck it into a bag or pocket to help keep you mindful of your goals and energy wherever you go.

What habits have you formed that took time to bear fruit? How long did they take and why? What habits are you forming that still need time or have further to go?

SPELL FOR WORKING WITH THE FULL MOON

This is the most well-known phase. The shining light of the Full Moon, bright and vibrant in the dark of the night, appears throughout ancient traditions, family lore, and pop culture. Its power lies in the full illumination that gleams from this ever-changing orb. The Full Moon has associations with abundance, achievement, celebration, and gratitude. Use its power to illuminate your achievements and spark celebration. Offer mindful thanks for the abundance in the garden of your life. Savor the aroma of success, pull a few weeds, and continue your journey along life's garden path.

For a Full Moon spell, look for ways to infuse the blessing of the fruits of your hard work into the process of clearing what no longer serves the full bloom of your intentions. Place a bowl of water under the Full Moon overnight—outdoors or in an open window, weather permitting. Bottle this water, full of generous lunar energy, to use for cleansing items for your altar or in a ritual bath. For a Full Moon bath that harnesses the generous energy of this part of the cycle, add cedar, cypress, or jasmine to the bath as well. These earthy, highly aromatic herbal allies support grounding and gratitude.

List below what in your life, at this moment, fills you with gratitude and why. Include items both big and small, related to your full moon intentions but also beyond them to whatever gives you joy, pleasure, and satisfaction. Create a document that celebrates the generous and joyful and return to it whenever you feel low.

SPELL FOR WORKING WITH THE WANING MOON

After the Full Moon, its light slowly ebbs, and the Moon grows smaller and darker. This cycle mirrors your life, with blooming and fallow moments, times of triumph followed by periods of quiet. This time of growing reflections gives you an opportunity to reflect and reassess any methods, habits, or processes that no longer serve you after the cycle of growth.

WANING GIBBOUS

As the light slips away, reflect and refine your approach, based on lessons learned. Draw on this waning phase to tidy up after the harvest. Assess what grew well and what needed extra tending to reach maturity. Where is nurturing still needed to complete plans before the cycle ends?

LAST QUARTER MOON

Acknowledge, release, and forgive. This phase offers the chance to acknowledge that life isn't perfect and to weed out negativity holding you back. Forgive anyone and everyone you choose—even yourself. Life is short. Let it go.

WANING CRESCENT

As the cycle ends and the Moon approaches the new phase, renew your intentions and reflect in quiet darkness. Listen to your heart and align your priorities. Review your garden, putting plants to bed as they finish their time in preparation for another growing season. Release and remove anything that doesn't fill you with energy and joy, be it a job, energy-stealing friends, useless possessions, unproductive worries, or negative self-talk. Position yourself to begin a new phase with a new goal and a refreshed attitude.

For a Waning Moon spell, especially in the darkness between the Waning Crescent and the New Moon, use your Full Moon water to cleanse your energy in preparation for the New Moon and new intentions. Pour some Full Moon water into a wide, shallow bowl filled with cleansing herbs. Peppermint (any mint), yarrow, lemon balm, or echinacea make excellent options, and you can combine them as you like. Dip your fingers or hands in the water while speaking aloud what you want to release into the Universe. Use this water to hydrate your plants and give your undesired energy back to the earth for respectful disposal.

In preparation for the next new moon, write a list of what you want to release: items, feelings, habits, even people. Write down not only what they are but also how they have served you in the past and why they no longer do. Allow the spirit of gratitude to guide your reflections.

PHASE 1, NEW MOON

A new beginning: The New
Moon's phase is like tilling the
soil to unlock its fertile potential.
Assess what's needed to amend it
to put forth a rich harvest.

PHASE 3,
FIRST QUARTER MOON

Stronger vibrations sharpen
intentions and intuition: Feel
the Moon's vibrations stir your
energies, taking root to grow
full and strong.

PHASE 2,
WAXING CRESCENT

Growing light awakens
intentions: The growing energies
of this Moon's phase stir activity.
Set your intentions and plant
their seeds to sprout.

PHASE 4,
WAXING GIBBOUS

Increasing excitement and
energy spur action: In the Moon's
growing light, celebrate new
growth and positive change
as your intentions, like your
growing herbs, show their
promise and begin to reward
your hard work.

PHASE 5, FULL MOON

Abundance, achievement, celebration, gratitude; also a time of letting go: Use the power of the Full Moon to illuminate your achievements and spark celebration. Offer mindful thanks for the abundance and savor the aroma of success.

PHASE 7, LAST (THIRD) QUARTER MOON

Acknowledge, release, forgive: Acknowledge that life is not perfect, weed out any negativity holding you back, and forgive anyone and everyone—even yourself! Let it go! Life is short.

PHASE 6, WANING GIBBOUS

Reflection, refining based on lessons learned: Draw on this waning phase to help tidy up after the harvest. Assess what grew well and what may have needed a little extra tending to reach maturity.

PHASE 8, WANING CRESCENT

The cycle ends—renew and reflect in quiet darkness: Listen to your heart and align your priorities. Release and remove anything that does not fill you with energy and joy. Position yourself to begin a new phase with a new goal and a refreshed attitude.

FALL

Fading light and blooms herald fall, but with it comes refreshing crispness and a special abundance of its own. The changing temperatures and shifting colors bring changes to the garden, but it still can teem with life and beauty. In your own life, you have times of preparation and transition. The garden behaves no differently, and this season gives you a moment to turn to the needs of the soil and the excitement of change.

Collect the bounty of the hard work you have invested into your garden since early spring, enjoy its fading vibrancy, gather seeds, and look forward to another spring by sowing what needs a deep chill to bring forth early flowers. Plants with a strong sense of agency will sow themselves as they like, but you have a final chance to plant cool-weather plants to keep the garden lively until the first frosts.

As the days grow shorter and colder, a turning inward takes place. Herbal allies that need a little extra protection should move into more sheltered environments. Relationships move to the forefront, those with your herbal allies and with other people. This transitional moment also offers a final chance to save and preserve the beautiful bounty of the summer and fall for the quiet, colder months.

A Guide to Preserving

As bounty expands and the harvest approaches, revisit how you might preserve the wonders of your garden for the colder months in anticipation of a gardenless period.

DRYING

This is by far the most approachable method. Hang bunches of trimmed herbs out of direct sunlight and with good air circulation until they dry fully. Once they have dried completely, you can process them by pulling them off the stems and saving them in a jar for year-round use.

SAUCES

Not a permanent fix unless you're ready to explore the thorny world of canning. You can turn fruits and herbs into sauces and store them in the fridge, though. Turning a sweet fruit into a jam keeps it useful and tasty for weeks. Turn savory herbs into a pesto and top with oil, which also will keep in the fridge for several weeks.

SOLUTIONS

Delicate herbs sometimes do best with minimal processing. Steeping edible ones in a syrup (1 part sugar dissolved in 1 part piping-hot water) will create a sweet botanical addition to teas and baked goods. Steeping them in a high-alcohol mixture, such as vodka or gin, will allow you to add their botanical flavor and benefits to cocktails, hot drinks, and other recipes. You also can add them to your favorite wine, steeping at room temperature, shaking frequently, and storing chilled after opening.

FREEZING

If you have a garden, you probably have access to a good freezer, a boon when dealing with an onslaught of vegetables. To freeze them best, blanche them lightly before storing. Grind herbs in a food processor with a glug or two of oil and freeze the mixture in an ice cube tray for later use.

SEEDS

As plants depart their green and fruiting season, they produce seeds in heads and pods of all sorts. If you'd like to grow the plant again, save the seeds rather than buying them (again). When the pods or heads look a bit dried out, place a small paper bag around the top of the stems, tie the bag closed, and trim. This method contains the seeds as you remove the plant material and helps keep seeds neat and sorted for processing and later storing in labeled paper envelopes.

SPELL FOR CELEBRATING TRANSITION

Snipping or pruning herbs from your garden, from pots, or from the farmers' market or grocery store begins with gratitude. Honor the bounty brought forth from the earth for its pure magical, mysterious delight and for the energy, nourishment, and magic it lends to your life. When you can, replant what you harvest—whether the same or something new—to continue the cycle.

Use every inch of the leaves, blooms, and seeds for the purpose. There's nothing wrong with letting things sit, but you have many good reasons to dive in. Harvesting most herbs and vegetables prompts new growth, extending the life of your garden. Trimmings that aren't herbally useful can make compost to enrich your garden in the next spring and summer season. Harvesting seeds helps you carry the garden into the next cycle and allows you to control how and where your allies will grow next year, even if you decide to sow seeds in the fall for cold stratification and early spring growth.

Harvesting mindfully can act as a spell all its own. Take the time to tend to each plant, reflecting on successes and failures, making note of anything you'd do differently. Thank the plant for its hard work and for all the joy it has brought you. If you keep a gardening journal, note not just the hard botanical facts of growth and bloom but also the joys of scent and any visitors it attracted. This reflection will deepen your joyful experience of the transition into fall and commemorate the work that your plants and you have done together.

TIPS FOR HARVESTING

Herbs: Pick herb leaves before flowers develop on the plants. Gather on warm mornings, after the awakening kiss of dew has evaporated.

Flowers: Snip new blossoms a day or two after they bloom.

Seeds: Herbs' flavorful, potent energies reside in their seeds. Harvest seed heads when mostly brown and hardening but not yet burst, with as long a stem attached as you can.

This past growing season, what plants brought you the most joy and why? Which thrived most in their current locations, and which might need a spring change? What did you harvest the most? Reflect not just on your garden but also on any plants, trees, and wild spaces in your environment.

SPELL FOR TIME TRAVEL

Drying herbs, especially those you grow yourself, has numerous benefits. Any herbal magic, whether done on your altar or in your kitchen, benefits from the freshest materials, with energy properties at their highest. But using lots of fresh herbs in your everyday routine can prove expensive. Growing herbs offers a far less costly option than buying fresh at a market or store, though of course those options work perfectly fine, too. However you choose to harvest your herbs, preserving them for their longest life and use matters.

The most important consideration is ensuring herbs dry fully before storing, easily achieved with good air circulation and time. Moisture promotes mold and spoilage, not the outcome you want for all your hard work!

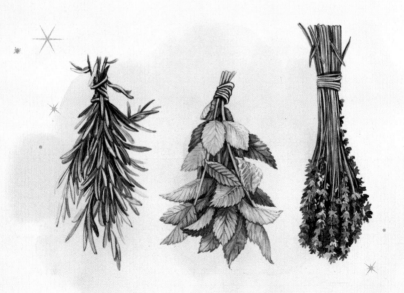

PREPARING HERBS FOR DRYING

After harvesting, you don't need to wash herbs grown organically. If you want to wash them, a quick rinse, shake, and thorough drying will suffice. Rinsing adds moisture, which we're trying to eliminate. Remove any dead, discolored, dirty, or wilted leaves before washing.

After harvesting, gather your herbs in small bundles and secure the stem ends either with rubber bands or twist ties. As the herbs dry, the bundle will shrink and the rubber band will loosen. Alternately you can tighten a twist tie to prevent the bundle from falling apart. You also can secure a thin cloth, like muslin, or a paper bag cut with air holes, over the bundle to catch any leaves or bits that fall from the bundle.

Sturdier herbs, such as rosemary and thyme, air-dry easily. Tender herbs, such as basil, mint, and lemon balm, have more moisture and take longer. Enclosing these types of herbs in a paper bag also helps absorb some of the moisture.

Hang the bundles by their stems in a dry, well-ventilated place: usually not the kitchen but somewhere you still can enjoy their energy, scent, and beauty. They will need about two weeks, maybe longer, to dry thoroughly. They're ready when they sound crunchy when crushed.

STORING DRIED HERBS

Storing herbs properly preserves their culinary and magical properties longer and honors the work you've done in harmony with nature to tend and nurture them to maturity—or the investment of money and time to source your herbs responsibly if you can't grow them yourself. Protecting them from moisture, sunlight, and air is key.

Remove the dried leaves from the stems and discard the stems. You can store the leaves whole or crumble them, as you wish, but whole herbs last longer. Remove the seeds from the seed heads or pods. You may want to work over a baking sheet or parchment paper to catch the leaves and seeds as they fall. Remove husks from seeds, as needed, by gently rubbing the seeds between your hands.

Store the leaves, seeds, or flowers separately in airtight containers in a cool, dark place to preserve their aroma and color. They will keep for 6 to 12 months.

When you're ready to cast a spell with your dried herbs, harken back to the days of magical living when drying was the standard method of preservation to prevent damage to valued tools. For a spell to evoke the warmer months, bundle small bouquets of favorite scented herbs. Rather than leaving them loose at one end, bind the whole length and use the guidelines above to dry the bundle into an incense packet. Make it small and narrow, no more than the length and width of a finger. Burn it on your altar in cold weather to recall the vibrant energy of the warmer months and to experience a connection to your garden year round.

Look around your altar or home for herbs from the past, either that you dried yourself or that came to you that way. Select a meaningful bouquet, bundle, or packet and try to remember as many details about how it came into your life as possible: its origins, the weather, how you felt before it entered your life, how it made you feel, and so on. As you connect fully with that past moment, record your memories below.

What herbs do you associate with certain periods of time before you were born and also from your past? Note them below. Do those associations stem from times of growth, harvest, or maybe a mix of both? What personal connections do you have to these herbs? What are they telling you about the past?

SPELL FOR CONNECTING WITH ANCESTORS

Since before recorded history, all cultures and civilizations have employed herbal practices for food, food preservation, spiritual purposes, and healing. Herbs have been sharing their magical lessons for millennia. They are perhaps the oldest magical tools available, their great secrets closely guarded. The origins of herbal magic lie in the centuries-old traditions of ancient healers, tribal shamans, wise women, and others who incorporated herbs with ritual work and prayer to cure and protect.

The ancient Egyptians organized schools for herbal study as long ago as 3000 BCE. The Eurasian spice trade dates back about four thousand years, with cinnamon one of the earliest traded spices. Traders guarded its origins so closely that they told fantastical tales of its procurement to reduce competition. Europeans cultivated herb gardens in the Middle Ages. The powerful culinary properties of herbs and spices became stock in trade. Some, like black pepper, became so revered or desired that they were available only to the wealthiest, and possession became a status symbol among the elite in medieval Europe.

Herbs nicely encapsulate the four classical elements: water, earth, fire, air. Planted in the earth, warmed by the sun, caressed by the wind, and quenched with water, each herb mingles its hereditary energies to begin its magical journey. The incredibly versatile combination of the earth and her gifts, you and your gifts, and a deep connection to herbal magic can enhance an already magical life or bring one into bloom.

You likely have an ancestor who liked to garden or cook with herbs. If no one comes to mind, do some digging. Look for people in your life or to your role models who demonstrate a deep connection to the plant world. Place their names, images, or both on your altar and call on their strengths in the herbal world and in life to fortify your own. If they are available to you, connect with them to learn about their own experiences and journeys. Your own story includes a strong connection to plants, and you can carry it forward by documenting your relationship and sharing your knowledge, becoming a good ancestor yourself.

What ancestors have influenced your relationship to herbs and plants and how? Who in your life continues to share plant wisdom with you?

Whom have you already taught about plants? What garden wisdom that you possess would you like to share with others in the future and why? Who in your life has shown an interest in learning more about your garden and the garden of your life? How can you better connect with that person or those people to share your knowledge?

SPELL FOR NOURISHING

One of the great joys of herbal gardening is sharing the magic with others. When you reach a point of having more bounty than you can consume or save for yourself, think through the best ways to share it and your magic with others.

It can be nice to share bunches of fresh herbs and flowers, but it's often more practical to employ a bit more preparation. At your fingertips, you have an enormous variation of ways to prepare your herbs for sharing. Preparation also provides an opportunity to infuse a little more intention and magic into this gift to bless your family, friends, and neighbors. You can share them, if perishable, immediately or save more shelf-stable preparations for gifts during the winter holidays.

Spread a little magic around by transforming your kitchen into a magical dispensary and your spell jars into edible gifts. Create custom labels conveying your message and fill the jars with your magic, fixing your blessings and intentions to the contents. The labels should help recipients identify both the items within and their purpose. Some ideas to get you started:

- apple butter for family harmony and love or good wishes for fame
- tea blends for a variety of wishes and dreams
- flavored salts, such as with dried rosemary for remembrance or thyme for beauty, protection, happiness, and good health, or a combination of those two herbs, sage, and lavender for a mixture of their magical properties
- infused syrups for an alcohol-free addition to drinks
- infused spirits, such as vodka or gin, for warming body and soul
- infused syrups and spirits together for a tasty cordial
- infused vinegars or oils for various intentions, as desired
- herbal pestos not limited only to basil (which does have significant powers in love and for protection)
- nuts spiced with cinnamon or black pepper to offer protection and to welcome new neighbors, show gratitude, or accompany a magical cocktail party

What herbal gifts have you encountered in your own life?—items purchased, given to you, or made. What might you make from your own herbal allies at hand? If you aren't growing any at the moment, what in your pantry might work toward this use?

SPELL FOR CULTIVATING GRATITUDE

As the growing seasoning comes to a close, think through what was most helpful, joyful, rewarding, or successful. Many plants continue to grow vigorously to and through the final frost. If you have access to a greenhouse or cold-frames, you can extend your gardening season into winter. You may even be able to grow in your local environment year round.

But do slow down and take stock of how your gardening season has gone. Celebrate your successes. As a plant ally, you always will have chores to do: houseplants need fertilizing and repotting, window boxes need preparing for winter, beds need clearing out and trimming back. Each season has its chores, allowing you to focus on and appreciate the present.

To ground yourself and connect to the coming winter season, cast a fire spell. At dusk or after the sun has set, stand in your garden space or before a window, wherever you connect with plants. On an even, stable surface, set out a fireproof dish and a lit candle. With a pen, write down on a piece of paper as many helpful, joyful, rewarding, or successful points you can think of about the growing months: growing life, green leaves, bright blooms, beautiful scents. When you have finished, thank the season aloud. Set the paper alight with the candle, with gratitude front of mind, and watch it burn completely to ash in the dish. Plant the ashes in your garden or in a potted plant.

What would you like to thank your garden for? What can you offer it in return?

SPELL FOR CLEARING SPACE

However green or black your thumbs, a time comes every year to clear space in your herbal library for fresh volumes and fresh energy. This task becomes especially important if you've spent the green months drying and preserving your bounty. You may think of the spaces you occupy as inert, not full of the life and energy that a garden has, but your home possesses its own energy. As you prepare for more time indoors and for reliance on what you've stored, take stock.

On a mild, early winter day, open all the windows and give your home a big, deep clean, as you would for spring cleaning. Clean areas where you grow or store plant materials especially well because, with less fresh air, overwatered plants are susceptible to mold. Stored materials can mold too. To clear your stores for success, turn your open-window day into a ritual cleaning by setting an intention, lighting a candle, and spreading a space-clearing scent that will bless your space with its energy.

Use this checklist for how to bring fresh energy to your space and make sure you're getting the most from your herbal stores:

- Clear out old syrups or preparations from your refrigerator—and toss any food or condiments past their prime, too.

- Compost any dried herbs more than a year old, especially if you dried them at home.

- Look over your houseplants and top their containers with fresh soil. Repot any that have outgrown their vessels.

- Process, jar, and label any dried herbs, discarding any that may have been forgotten or gathered dust.

- Remove any produce stored in your crisper or root storage, washing the spaces if necessary.

What new routines are you anticipating in the indoor season and why? What plans to rest and recharge are you formulating while your plants do the same?

SPELL FOR PROTECTION & LUCK

Throughout the ages, witches and wily folk have used herbalism to court fortune and favor. The brews they made went by many names and still persist in homes, botánicas, and herbalist shops. One such simple concoction that you can make at home traces its history to the time of the Black Death. Known as thieves' vinegar or Marseilles vinegar, this ultimate DIY kitchen magic offers a welcome tonic for today's turbulent times.

Reputedly developed in the seventeenth century by a band of thieves to protect against sickness and harm as they looted the dead in France, it combined the cleansing attributes of vinegar with the herbal properties of "wormwood, meadowsweet, wild marjoram, sage, 50 cloves, 2 ounces of campanula roots, 2 ounces of angelic[a], rosemary, horehound, and 3 large measures of camphor," according to René-Maurice Gattefossé, the father of aromatherapy.

The use of potions containing vinegar and herbs to ward off illness dates to centuries earlier, but their secret lies in the antiviral properties of the vinegar and antibacterial properties of the herbs. The concoction also apparently repelled fleas, a suspected carrier of plague. A regular dousing kept the bandits healthy, but it didn't prevent their arrest, upon which they credited their health to the potion and bartered the recipe for their freedom—or so legend says.

With a base of apple cider vinegar, today's recipes vary widely, but their purpose remains the same: protection from all kinds of evil (including the common cold). Modern combinations often call for black pepper, cinnamon, clove, garlic, juniper, lavender, rosemary, sage, and thyme. To make your own tonic to address whatever plagues you, gather:

- 1 head garlic, cloves halved or roughly chopped

- 2 tablespoons each of 4 herbs, fresh or dried, plus additional herbs as desired for flavor or intention

- 4 cups (960 ml) organic apple cider vinegar

In a clean quart-size (960 ml) jar, combine the garlic and herbs. Pour in the vinegar, almost to the top of the jar. Use a wooden spoon to stir the mixture, coaxing out any air bubbles. Place a piece of parchment paper over the mouth of the jar and seal the lid. Let its magical properties multiply (where you normally store your vinegars) for about a month, shaking daily to distribute the herbs. Strain the vinegar into a clean jar, pressing the herbs to extract as much of their essence as possible, and seal the new jar. Compost the herbs if possible and thank the earth for their healing properties.

Use this potion as an edible spell in any recipe calling for vinegar: a dressing for a ritual meal, mixed to taste into sparkling water, dabbed behind your ears in a nod to the thieves, or as a natural cleaning solution (first testing surfaces to ensure the acid in the vinegar doesn't damage them).

What spaces in your home could use an energetic pick-me-up? List them below and create an herbal plan to clear or refresh the vibrations in each space.

Consider hosting a feast of thieves that pays tribute to the bandits of yore. Create a menu below that incorporates your new tonic. What other dishes would you serve and why?

SPELL FOR HOPEFUL FUTURES

The days are growing shorter, but there's still gardening to do. While the air develops a chill and plants begin to die back, opportunities for joy abound. Many seeds and plants require cold weather to help their seeds germinate or come back earlier in the spring if sown later in the fall. These herbs don't mind a cool fall planting and potentially can overwinter for early spring growth:

- anise
- caraway
- chervil
- cilantro / coriander
- mint
- oregano
- parsley
- sage
- thyme

Fall is also the time to plant bulbs for spring color and annual flowers that need cold to put them to sleep for waking when warmth returns. Many wildflowers, bulb flowers, and colorful non-edibles don't have a strong place in herblore, but they still form an important part of the ecosystem, supporting a variety of pollinators, for example. Always check that a bulb or other plant isn't considered invasive to your area. These bright bulbs overwinter happily:

- bluebell
- crocus
- fritillaria
- hyacinth
- lily of the valley
- trillium
- tulip

You can sow wildflowers in open areas or containers—but not in your vegetable or herb beds, where they can act as weeds! Again, confirm that nothing you sow is invasive. Research your local pollinators and the local plants they love, such as:

- bachelor's buttons
- bluebonnets
- cosmos
- flax
- lupines
- poppies
- sweet peas
- zinnias

When you sow anything in the fall, treat it as a ritual for a bright, fruitful, joyful future after the winter months. Use the process of marking containers and beds, sowing, and recording your plans for reference in the summer as a manifestation spell that you can touch and feel.

What flowers and plants are still growing and blooming where you are? What plants are full of life, and which have begun to fade?

....

....

....

....

....

....

....

....

....

....

....

....

....

....

SPELL FOR MARKING ENDINGS

It's natural to feel a little sad and tender as a garden declines for the season, just as it's normal to mourn when any good thing comes to an end. Rituals of commemoration form an important part of magic practice, and fall offers a wonderful time to seek ways to connect to the cycles of the seasons, full of endings and beginnings. As the growing season winds down into flaming reds, oranges, and yellows, take time, apart from chores, to reconnect with your garden. As the air grows crisp and days grow short, spending time with your plants will help your heart and mind prepare for the coming chill.

Sit wherever you can immerse yourself in a familiar, natural space: a favorite wooded path, your garden, or a window full of potted plants. Settle yourself comfortably in a sunny spot that allows you to observe the natural world around you, which might include your neighbors or other humans. Remember that we all belong to nature. Take a deep breath and attend to the smell of the air. Focus on how it feels to bring the outside world into your lungs. Exhale and feel the movement within you rejoin the world. Repeat this cycle, breathing evenly and securely, slowly expanding your awareness to feel the air on your skin and any movement around you. Let the moment fill your senses and etch it into memory. Thank Mother Nature for allowing you to accompany her on another cycle and for welcoming you into her period of rest.

When do you make time for rest and connection in your routine? What natural cycles of ebb and flow are present in your life? How can you channel their energies to bring more calm and peace into your life?

WINTER

*A*t first, you need to keep busy during this time to rest and plan. You'll have garden chores to do to ensure a successful spring. Then come the frosts, and all you can do is wait. So cut back and arrange the plants to make it through the short Persephone days until spring reemerges.

In this fallow period, begin dreaming long before any bulbs emerge. Catalogues of seeds will become available, and if you have access to a greenhouse or even a small heat lamp and grow light, you can make lists of what to start before spring approaches. Ultimately the winter months, full of potential energy and unconstrained by practicality, test a gardener's patience.

An underappreciated part of a garden's life cycle, rest truly is necessary. Even environs not sunk deep in snow need it to recover from spending energy and to nurture seeds set out after the wild, generous, green months. Without dedicated downtime, nothing escapes burnout or exhaustion. Your life requires this time of quiet reflection as well. When better to embrace it than when the natural world does the same?

A Guide to Garden Planning

DREAM BIG

Winter harbors latent energy. Everything in the garden resets, and you can reevaluate and reinvest your energy. Don't let past failures dampen your spirits; you learn so much every time you try! Bring your biggest dreams to the table and don't be afraid if they take more than one green season to achieve.

CONSIDER THE PAST

If you've been documenting your gardening, review your successes and anything you'd like to change when you try again in the spring. If one particular plant refuses to thrive in your space, don't hold tight to that particular variety. Release it from its struggles and look for variations better suited to your space and conditions or another plant that will prosper.

INCORPORATE REST

Some plants need to rest. Any plants taken indoors for the winter likely will experience a still or fallow period, in which they appear to be in stasis. Those outside may look entirely unrecognizable in the winter or disappear entirely. Have faith that rejuvenation will follow rest and that the quiet period will restore both you and your garden.

DO YOUR RESEARCH

While a good time for rest and review, winter also provides a great time for planning what comes next. With no plants to water or seedlings to tend, nothing to weed or harvest, you can fantasize freely about new plants or new methods.

HAVE PATIENCE

The number-one way in which most gardeners self-sabotage is impatiently desiring an early spring. Pay attention to timing and don't rush your seedlings or planting at the first sign of a thaw. Most last-frost dates fall much later than any gardener wants, so heed local cycles. If in doubt, wait a bit.

SPELL FOR EASING WORRY

A spell sachet can work in soft and cozy surfaces, a perfect magical tool to aid sleep and rest. As with an herbal spell jar, you can fill the muslin or sachet bags with crystals, flowers, dried herbs, and other energy boosters to create dream bags or charm bags. Cast your intentions into it and place one under your pillow to induce sweet dreams, carry it with you for ongoing spellwork toward manifestation, or give it as a gift to add a little magical boost to someone's life.

- angelica, garlic, mistletoe, or Himalayan salt to increase feelings of safety, security, and protection
- basil for money woes
- cardamom to stir feelings of love, lust, and, if jealousy rules your heart, fidelity
- chamomile for restful sleep
- dill or fennel to quiet bad dreams in children
- dried acorns to reverse worries about aging
- geranium to help ease tension in the body
- ginger to relieve the effects of general stress
- hops to hop on the dreamland express
- lavender to quiet the mind and promote positive feelings
- lemon balm to clear the cobwebs
- marigold if legal troubles loom large
- motherwort to press pause on panic
- passionflower to ease chronic worry
- peppermint to soothe tensions and headaches
- rose petals for love woes and healing

- rosemary to boost the healing love received from others and rejuvenate energy if stress is sapping yours
- sage to ease grief
- St. John's wort to lift depression
- star anise for feelings of calm and protection from the evil eye
- thyme to help you feel grounded
- verbena to promote peaceful feelings
- violet to let go of frustration
- ylang-ylang to reduce anxiety and improve libido

In your life, what are your natural periods of rest, and how do you recharge? Do you have a favorite place or time to do so? Note them below.

SPELL FOR WARMING THE HEART

Dating to ancient China and Egypt, herbal tea, or a tisane—an infusion made with any edible part of a plant, such as leaves, seeds, bark, blossoms, or roots—has a long, worldwide history of use for health, healing, and spiritual purposes. Purists argue that any tea not made with *Camellia sinensis*—from which traditional black, green, and oolong varieties come—doesn't count as true tea. Therefore, you sometimes will hear herbal teas called "botanical infusions" or "tisanes." Designating a spot in your herbal magic plot for tea—a section of your garden, a pot on the windowsill, or an intentional purchase from a farmers' market or online—can prove both calming and inspiring.

The herbs listed below are easy to find and grow, and most are also easy to find in tea blends, so you can try them in cold months and plant out what you like best. They will entice you into the garden, then onto the porch or into your favorite chair to relax and rejuvenate. Infuse a cup to help with whatever troubles or calls you. Infusions generally use leaves and blossoms, which imbue the water with their essential oils, aromas, and flavors.

BASIL (LEAVES):
floral, licorice flavor; love, money spells, protection

CHAMOMILE (BLOSSOMS):
apple-honey flavor; comfort, patience, sleep

ECHINACEA (BLOSSOMS):

strong, tongue-tingling, straw-like flavor; inner strength, immunity

LEMON BALM (LEAVES):

herbal lemony flavor; sympathy

HIBISCUS (BLOSSOMS):

fruity, floral flavor; attracting love, moon magic, intuition

LEMON THYME AND COMMON THYME (LEAVES):

herbal lemon flavor; woodsy, pungent; beauty, courage, good health, prevent nightmares, protection, remove negative energy, sleep

LAVENDER (BLOSSOMS):

sweet floral, herbal flavor; cleansing, devotion, peace, calm, intelligence, happiness

LEMON VERBENA (LEAVES AND BLOSSOMS):

lemon-lime flavor; inspiration

MINT (LEAVES):
cooling, slightly peppery; clear and meaningful communication, refreshment, travel

ROSEMARY (LEAVES):
strong pine-like flavor; clarity, remembrance, sweet dreams, purification

PASSIONFLOWER (LEAVES):
mild grassy, floral flavor; relaxation, soothes strong emotions, hospitality

ST. JOHN'S WORT (BLOSSOMS):
mildly bitter; easing depression, serenity

ROSE (HIPS, SPENT BLOOMS):
sweet floral flavor; immunity boost, love

To make the perfect cup, whether purchasing dried or fresh herbs or using herbal allies grown in your garden, always choose organic for their purity. As a general rule, use 2 to 3 teaspoons of dried herbs for every 8 ounces (240 ml) of boiling water. For larger quantities, say a 1-gallon (3.8 L) jar, start with about 1 cup of dried herbs. Some herbs are stronger than others, so experiment to find the perfect ratio for your tastes and the herbs that you prefer. For fresh herbs, toss a large handful, to taste, into a teapot; loose, in a strainer; or in an eco-friendly, unbleached tea bag. Cover the herbs with boiling water and let steep for at least 5 minutes, or longer as desired. Sweeten the tea with dried fruits, spices, or honey. Serve hot or cold, as you like.

Use your tea as a powerful potion to correspond with a moon phase, for spellwork, or to relax for a spell. Close your eyes, inhale the aromas and energies from the plants, and meditate, even for just a few seconds, on your intentions. Now exhale them into action. Incorporate a spell for abundance and expand your tisane repertoire along with your herbal wisdom.

What is your favorite herbal tea blend and why? What elements of it can you add to your garden in the coming spring? What herbs have you grown already that you can use to make your own tea blend?

SPELL FOR SOOTHING A BROKEN HEART

Love lost brings a special kind of pain that, like nature, takes its own time to heal. Herbal allies can soothe, but they can't fix what happened. They support you and provide comfort while you work on dissolving the heartache that you feel. Think of what gives you the most comfort when facing a challenge or struggling with a problem. For some, a cup of tea provides the ultimate self-care; for others, a long run, walk, or bath soothes the soul. Whether you choose pampering or nourishing your body—or maybe both—you can choose from a rich variety of helpful herbs: salt, rose, yarrow, lemon balm, nettle, or motherwort, for example. Any or all of them can help ease you through the process of repairing a broken heart.

If you need a tactile way to process your grief, call on bleeding heart, chives, dill, hawthorn, lavender, witch hazel, and yarrow. Put any or all in a tear jar, and use it to catch your tears as they fall—and don't forget to add rosemary to hold onto the happy memories. When the jar has filled and the tears evaporate, your heart will have healed.

Think back to a time when you thought your heart had broken forever but you recovered. What did you do to help support your healing process? What helped most and why?

What lost loves are you experiencing now or foresee in your future? When they come, how can you make space for your grief alongside your healing and hopes for the future?

SPELL FOR MAKING SPACE

An altar provides a visual reminder and a physical space to focus your energy, meditate, or try an herbal spell or two, indoors or outside. You can create more than one altar, imbuing each with a different purpose, such as attracting love, raising a healthy family, cultivating gratitude, or managing stress, for example. It doesn't have to be fancy and can be as simple as a windowsill or even a cardboard box. It can remain fixed in place, move around, or both. It might even be a shelf or dresser top where you display your plants, crystals, candles, and other reminders of your intentions to sow herbal magic in your life. Consider an altar in your kitchen with objects devoted to nourishment and health, one in your bedroom to promote sweet dreams or romance, or one in your herb garden to celebrate the charms and abundance that nature gives your world.

Once you decide on the best location, cleaning the space removes negative energy and makes room for good vibrations to flourish. Wipe it with rosemary or rose water and sweep it clean with a bundle of sage leaves. Decorate your altar as you wish; be as creative, fancy, or minimalist as you like. As much as possible, keep altar elements natural to make use of their innate individual energies. Cast your intentions and desires onto the altar as you gather and place each element.

You may wish to include a bowl of clean soil, a cup of water, Himalayan salt, crystals, or herb seeds to represent the earth and the magic you cultivate there. Place dried herbs, fresh flowers, seeds, spices, or plants to celebrate and magnify the energies your soul seeks. Set out candles in colors that support your intentions or use colored candleholders with white candles in them. Decorate your candles with dried herbs (burning them safely and mindfully) to add energy to energy. Display crystals with vibrational energies that connect with your goals. Incorporate essential oils based on what you need or for use in meditation, such as rose or frankincense. Pictures of loved ones or other reminders of those important to you will help focus your intentions and magic. Keep handy a deck of tarot cards, a scrying bowl, or other tools to assist in daily meditation or intention-setting. Write wishes on a bay leaf and place it on your altar to manifest. Include books that have special meaning. Keep spell jars, poppets, and herbal sachets on the altar or in sight to channel their magical vibrations.

Your altar represents you: your home, heart, hopes, dreams, intentions, and life. Change it for the seasons as your work with nature and your life's intentions grow and evolve. If you stay true to your heart, your altar will help you work your magic when you call upon it.

If you could put anything on an altar to honor where you are in your life right now, what items—flowers, herbs, colors, images, and objects—would you place and why?

SPELL FOR MAKING TIME

When drawing on herbal magic, thyme and timing can prove important to achieving the desired outcome. Herbal magic works when the need presents itself, but aligning your intentions with the proper herbal and universal energies will make your magic stronger. The power held in the vast, some say infinite, skies—home to gods and goddesses, other worlds, our sun and moon, other planets and their moons, the wisdom of ages—is wise, abundant, and available. You have only to look up.

Looking within yourself will reveal the secrets to living your best magical life on earth, but searching the skies for confirmation can increase the energy and vibration that will trigger, hasten, or otherwise influence your charms. Gardening frequently uses almanacs, which incorporate everything from astrology to weather patterns to recommend the best times for planting, harvesting, and all sorts of gardening tasks. If you garden in the same place each year, keep a gardening journal to track everything you notice about when it was too cold, too hot, or just right in your microclimate. If you're just starting, pick up a calendar and almanac and take some time in the winter to mark out when to expect the first thaw, last frost, and planting days. Mark, too, if you plan to start seedlings, buy plants, or do any pre-planting chores.

The rhythm of ritual and the magic of anticipation allow you to manipulate time. Winter passes quickly when you're looking not just for warm weather but planting weather. It also feels so much more precious and rich on its own merits of cozy planning and dreaming, of buying seeds and making plans. Craft a spell of anticipation by gathering your seeds and planning your garden in detail. Create a detailed plan that notes ideal planting times for each of the seeds or plants, when to harvest or cut them, and how to fill the spaces between meaningfully. Consult your local farmer's almanac and any previous experiences gleaned from your garden. Treat this mindful, yearly ritual as a charm for gardening success. Make sure to include herbs for good fortune, such as angelica, borage, bluebell, clover, huckleberry, ivy, Job's tears, olive, or violet.

What plants or garden additions are you looking forward to in the spring and why? When will you be able to act on those plans? What preparation do you need to do beforehand?

SPELL FOR KEEPING MEMORY

Repetition can turn any action into ritual, and intention can transform any ritual into a spell. The earth, the best teacher of this lesson, invites you to return to the same actions, rhythms, and rituals as your ancestors. It cycles, repeating every year, accumulating a rich compost of memory and routine. Each time new leaves emerge in the spring, it feels as joyful as if it had never happened, yet spring always follows winter, as regular as day comes after night.

When the gardening season ends, it's easy to let days and months blur in an unreliable haze of memory. While the garden remains fresh in your mind, write down your notes and thoughts about it. Depending on how you want to use these notes in the future, these can take the shape of formal reports; dated timelines of bloom, seed, and harvest; or, especially if you're working after the growing season has ended, more thoughtful reflections that linger on the successes as missteps and failures fade.

For now, take some time to meditate on the garden. Seat yourself comfortably and close your eyes, breathing evenly and deeply. Imagine in your mind's eye your gardening space, even if it's just a small windowsill. Envision the placement of the pots or beds, what's growing in them, each of the plants. Describe the scents and sounds of the garden, the colors, and the movement. When you finish, write everything you can remember about your garden in a notebook or on a piece of paper that you store with your gardening tools and plant materials. Return to the document the next time you return to your garden chores.

What were your favorite moments in the garden this year and why? What are you most looking forward to next year, and how can you participate or be fully present in that experience?

SPELL FOR FACING YOUR FEARS

Sometimes operating outside your comfort zone or a fear of failure can create uncomfortable feelings that freeze you in your tracks. If you feel that procrastination or not taking action comes from a deeper place, acknowledge it and face it. Take one deep breath and two steps forward and soon you will forget what was holding you back.

Herbal allies can help instill bravery and courage in your heart by nourishing your body and soul. But they also can draw your worries to them, anchoring them away from your body and freeing your energy for healing and moving forward. Gather any or all of these herbs for courage: basil, black pepper, borage, dandelion, garlic, holly, lavender, lemon thyme, motherwort, mullein, oregano, St. John's wort, tarragon, or violet. Place them in a vessel—a bottle, sachet, or altar dish—transfer your apprehension into this worry vessel and free your mind to resolve your fears.

When you feel consumed with any kind of anxiety, hold the vessel with both hands and envision yourself pouring your worries into the contained space. Allow yourself to feel the peaceful emptiness left inside you by exorcising these worries. When finished, place the vessel somewhere safe but out of sight. Return to it, as needed, whenever you need to create a space for calm within yourself.

Recall two or three different times that you faced your fears and triumphed. Think about them carefully. What went into each of your victories? How can you call on those strengths and channel those triumphs again in the future?

....

....

....

....

....

....

....

....

....

....

....

....

What herbal allies make you feel empowered and joyful and why?
Are they growing in your garden now? If not, how and when can you
bring them into your growing space?

SPELL FOR CLOSURE

When a cycle comes to a close, offer a sign of respect to mark its ending. Show your gratitude for your time in the green season by making an offering to the earth. You can do so in many ways, but the most important part of designing a closing ritual is ensuring that it holds meaning for you and the growing space to which you have bound yourself.

During the summer months, press flowers and plants to dry and save them. Also save interesting stones or branches, any natural item that comes from your surroundings that connects you to them. As a guideline, think about what you would put on an altar, then consider doing just that for this spell. If you don't have any items, don't worry. Go outside to look for likely items. Even one evergreen branch will do.

Once you've assembled your items, find a quiet place to sit and place them in a dish before you. Close your eyes and thank the earth for your bright time together this past season. Silently or aloud, as feels right, wish it a restful sleep. Open your eyes and bury your items outdoors, ideally in one of your garden beds, as a gift to your garden space.

What routines or rituals do you already use to mark endings in your garden, in the year, or in your life? How do they help you with closure and moving forward? What other rituals or routines would you like to consider trying?

SPELL FOR KEEPING THE FAITH

Building on the concept of a spell jar to capture intention (page 84), you can capture the gratitude and accomplishment present in the end of the growing season, as well as your own, in a similar way.

Gather a pen, small piece of paper, dry vessel or sachet, plus a blend of seeds that grow well together. They could be lettuces and greens, radishes, peas, wildflowers, or an herb mix, anything that can be planted at the same time and in the same container. You also need a taper candle (the shape matters) ideally made of beeswax. You can include other meaningful items, but bag your seeds before placing them in the jar or sachet so you can plant them later.

On the paper, write as many good memories from your garden as you can recall or your hopes for next spring. Roll the paper into a scroll and place it inside your vessel or sachet with your seeds and any other meaningful items. Put the energy of your gardening year into the jar and cover it. You can charge and magnify this vessel by placing it under a full moon, meditating while holding it, or even placing it in the garden overnight if it's still relatively mild outside. Once the vessel has charged, light the candle and carefully seal the edge of the vessel with wax. Place the spell jar in a safe place with your gardening supplies to await spring. Hold it when you need a reminder that spring will come again, sooner than you think.

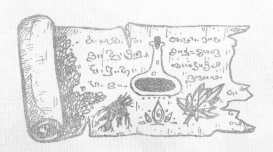

What have your garden and your plants taught you about cycles?
What will you take forward into the next year of gardening?

© 2022 by Quarto Publishing Group USA Inc.

First published in 2022 by Wellfleet Press, an imprint of The Quarto Group,
142 West 36th Street, 4th Floor, New York, NY 10018, USA
T (212) 779-4972 www.Quarto.com

Wellfleet titles are also available at discount for retail, wholesale, promotional, and bulk
purchase. For details, contact the Special Sales Manager by email at specialsales@quarto.com
or by mail at The Quarto Group, Attn: Special Sales Manager, 100 Cummings Center Suite 265D,
Beverly, MA 01915 USA.

10 9 8 7 6 5 4 3

ISBN: 978-1-57715-292-7

Publisher: Rage Kindelsperger
Creative Director: Laura Drew
Managing Editor: Cara Donaldson
Cover and Interior Design: Amelia LeBarron
Text: Mary J. Cassells and Haley Houseman

Printed in China